CUSP

FOR LYN
love Jocelyn

Jocelyn Saidenberg

D1017643

THE FRANCES JAFFER BOOK AWARD

KELSEY ST. PRESS

Some of these writings have appeared in *Aufgabe, Clamour, Kenning, Outlet, Primary Writing* and *Tripwire*. Thanks to the editors of these publications.

A special thanks to Bob Glück and Rob Halpern for their generous readings of this work.

This award for the publication of a first book honors the memory of Bay Area poet, editor and feminist Frances Jaffer, 1921–1999.

Judge: Barbara Guest

Library of Congress Cataloging-in-Publication Data

Saidenberg, Jocelyn.
   Cusp / Jocelyn Saidenberg.
      p. cm.
   ISBN 0-932716-58-X (alk. paper)
      I. Title.

   PS3569.A374 C85 2001
   811'.54–dc21

                              2001050379

Series design by Poulson/Gluck Design

Text is set in 10 point New Baskerville.
Printed in an edition of 600.

All orders to: Small Press Distribution
                        800-869-7553   email: orders@spdbooks.org

Please note: We do not read unsolicited manuscripts for this award.

You can visit Kelsey St. Press online at: www.kelseyst.com

CONTENTS

Publication of this book was made possible, in part, by a generous grant from the Greenwall Fund of The Academy of American Poets.

CUSP

SEANCE

This was a history of her. Perhaps she never came really to have it in her, perhaps she came to have it a little in her, always some one was working in her for her, this is a history of her.

The Making of Americans, Gertrude Stein

VENTILATION

travels the length of it down into it—some color. as
inevitable as our nervous system. the color being near by it
or nearer to it. a second circumference. and then down
exists indefinitely. i dose myself with the pleasure of the lost
myself. my veins run through it—a crack shudders in the
garden wall. a cycled cell. another incident. i swear it
then down.

he said he came by water with her
anti-gravitational heart. wherein
we recite an a priori no.

we landed learned to swim and prepared
for our trip to the south polar regions. we reveal ourselves
all of many parts. excellent tosspots. bad airs make me
choke. a certain diseased taint and a flight into wilderness.
we are surrounded.

no family banners to plant. in the countryside that
worn-out countryside. stealing the experience again and
again i discover.

that pink moment in that pink corridor folded into a pink
attitude of longing both pink and filthy. a pink. a second
life. in its sunny brilliance its distance its spaciousness its
certainty its
immensity.

TWIST IT

she: her doelike throat her circumscribed habits. he:
the habits of one habitually bored who cares none for those

2

who care not about anything. i am constantly on guard.
answer yes to the following questions—held in place by a
set of ordered numbers. genus species families. satellites.
we are tired. tried. triad. who bites no longer.

their clothes stink of them their thoughts stink of them their
laughter and failures both stink of them make them heroes
—heroic.

in a dimwitted way. the carnival owners—they keep going
no matter where i go. reproducing more freaks. where i
don't go. endless pleasure. endless in my mind. we closed
ranks to struggle all against all.

INNER SHUDDER

> someday we will
> look back at this
> and laugh.

a drunken inner shudder. jubilant and closer to the bone.
living without a yes without a no. that which it depends on—
as in the desert in a filing cabinet. algebraic in construction
subtracting the track. wanting us breaking.

a feeling of contempt for. castigation. thinned. thready
hair falling out on the subway. into a place as print surfaces.
to change or convey. by means of a bus or train or the like.

a ticket entitling the person a passenger. that goes on into
correspondence. convert wishes into deeds or a mechanical
body. on to more rotation from one place to another
without to halting—excuse me

exalting.

a parenthetical yoo-hoo. if we had
had these when we were young we
would have killed so much more
nothingness. it was glorious.
having never had the occasion to
look down ira's oral cavity.

a weed study—the fist. insistent communication
with that which finds pleasure in self-exposure. toy with
our dreams. the headlessman and the shuttle. nuclear
encyclopedia. exists and then fails again. regroups and fails
again and then fails again.

a splinter and spread it out over as many parts. the i eating.
the he somehow related to the she and the i. cellular. horns
on all of our heads. irrespective of any particular less than
reliable little glow worm. misadventures with a hat maker.
cast down another limb.

a weapon or a pen to violate as fluid. a nonsense rescue
attempt at the limits of say kindness in elevation. saying no
again to whatever would be dished up. radios and radars—
rays of light beyond a sheer point. seeping in and very
spendable.

suppressing all
details. destroying
the toy to reach its
heart.

strange period after revolution or the decline of great

reigns. no gallant heroism but an elegant dressed-up voice.

an age of activity hesitation and indolence mixed up with a

weariness with struggle vague enthusiasms and dazzling

utopias. as i retrace the details recitative with

bird trills — a task immobile and oneiric.

i was about to answer about to fall at
her feet about to offer her my life
when at that moment we arrived at.

the circumstances of this event which had

such a great effect on my life are of little importance now. a

second life — a shudder.

i will later try to explain why i did not choose her or even

her place of birth. her first complete words were *garbage*

truck and the place of her

birth.

reverie. the abyss itself.

the very spot on which we stood seemed to grow

and rise and lose its urban aspect. a night patrol soon

surrounded us. we were gentle with our strengths. i made

so much noise they put me in a cell. on the wall in front of

me hung a clock and on this clock was a painted bird who

spoke to me like a father.

either directly or innately they take the forms of animals so as silent observers. i myself wandered throughout the streets of a busy unknown city. she seemed to vanish in her own immensity. separated then joined again in an embrace cemented by human blood. forlorn and powerless.

it grew worse in the early morning hours. more so when i found i was tied down. sleep takes up one third of our lives. i never feel any rest there. for a few seconds numbed and then a new life begins freed from the conditions of time and space.

> exhaustion
> in immensity.

SQUARE PEG

> what   he   was
> winning he   was
> never   keeping.
> he can't keep.

an x-like strawman filled with leaves and sawdust. found digging again around in the dirt for something lost or trapped. a randomness of his own. he who was who was us dutiful and honest stuck in his castle—uniting the square pegs. boast and swagger.

vanishing into the maid's room with 3D cards—minds and legs of their own. the shuddering his trademark his monger.

protean oceanic number of the silent majority. pure and
unspotted. by-and-by breaking

> the main springs.

construct
the embrace.

> spreading the mountain. his perimeter—ubiquitous
> while censoring by proxy. agonistic. part this part that.
> losing his eyes and whiskers growing shabby. cast down the
> stones.

> > our no.
> > his yes.

his filthy bald spot lurking around the filthy bedpost in
what we came to call his filthy greenhouse of invention—
invection—brainwashing the filthy gridlock of the cell
walls. ideas do not grow on trees. what owes. filthy does.

why can't he smoke and play cards all the day long. rustling
leaf. causing the heaviness of his own transparency.
upgraded to an afterlife. the quiet evenings in the woods
sitting in the bracken watching the ants move to and fro.

for a long time he lived in the toy cupboard or on the
nursery floor. could not claim to model anything but
sawdust. a sawdust heart. his sawdust heart. no longer

> an elsewhere.

yearning toward these reveries
blank shapes on the map dim
specks—cold blots.

        i mean him in the background. state his
protection. he poaches on it. his rented room in his second
life. his borrowed space. he is liable to vanish again
diverting himself without leaving. intrudes himself—the
oceans filling in the cracks in the wall. an immense forest
the streets of his desires. objects without use. without us.
watching the crack run against the wall. introduces rotten
materials. odd machines. a relative communion.

REHEARSAL AFTERLIFE

        in your head. say
where you have
been.

especially. precisely not. in my head endlessly memorizing.
cordially lubricated ventilated. 100 places of pie. talking to
myself—a rehearsal. all over the world i am held in place
by self-discipline.

a butting of heavy with skipping. she threw it away like
a lighted display case. brainwashing foreclosure. my
perimeter—part this and then again part that. gridlocked.
so what does when used properly. a tiff effectively means of.
tested for reliability. belated. as you always come after.

mum's the word and deracinate—reroot.   cordial and
amiable. neither cordial nor amiable. relive the second life.
a dream a life-like seance. a chiasmatic story time. a rotten
egg. he is a good egg silently losing. placing the birth.
a cause. allergies electronically shudder. the world imprints
itself in wax. a cube rotating in space.

liable and spendable. reading aloud
heads that don't say NO heads that
are tossing to and fro in the night
air.

a ship sailing out of my brain—those southern
polar regions. highways tying cities together cutting the
world in twos. for all the aforementioned reasons. my
itinerant igloo. reduce reroot electric transmissions.

you are standing at your father's grave:
no answer
you are standing in the rain: no answer
standing at the window: listening: cutting the
world into ribbons.

PELL-MELL

my heart is freezing—it is time—things left undone.
immense things left undone flung under the bed. the
streets the words. drive us outside. restless in exhaustion.

these desires in my head these splinters these scissors of
desires these knives these razors of desires shudder my
brain. break my eardrums.

just false starts. you catch your death. catch your own death. deathlike. breathtaking—literally never beyond. feeble. always pretending a pretend enthusiasm. offend wherever we go. visiting the carnival owners—their ape's milk. when i leave they say nasty things slander me smear me with all manner of filthy words. neither correct nor amiable.

CUSP

What ere shee meant by'it, bury it with me

"The Funerall," John Donne

preferences. reference. partial things so said. how did we get here how did you or i. playing over and over again make numbers. more numbering cutting burning counting since we started.

she made the senses plain. used them to describe. how we come to predict her next words. how come. how parsimonious. how scented.

we resorted to walking again resemblances of an armory of thoughts. ill thoughts. a false bottom. armory of weapons. ill weapons. real? bottom?

as a.

as a head. gloms onto something. some thing else. someone else joining forces. joint forces? if joining were if joining might. might be our might tonight.

SYNDICATION

palpable tributaries

industrious toilings

messy points along her way

intolerable space?

plod and slog

will you assign seats?

a herculean commonplace

constructing the mobile

responsiveness in the move

all i ever wanted to be was a soldier

salt flats

i march on and pivot

and of us and of her hulk and of her span
or of her palm and with light with colors
we say always she did will always
and of her neck and on her lead and
names names we may always here she
will always always a thing here an ample it

speculation / emancipation
the third sex. a third sex?
temporary pacts

prattling on. give us something to do. we've done nothing to him we can't
do anything to him. we're innocent he's innocent nobody's fault? mouths
are dry. run dry. poor devils. this state of affairs. can't do anything. doing
my best and it's nobody's fault? thirsty again. keep coming forward keep
counting.

there are three of us sometimes five and then again four sometimes.
transport.
despite the mold.

we stop under infrequent trees.
utter utter. act this way. always she.
again we resorted to walking.

the need to bury things alive. to absent the thing in order to mean anything something some one. its unreliability. to show some fear. wade knee deep. wholesale. of the buried coming back to actually provide for. for itself mostly. stiff corpus deluxe. that form from which we are in flight and the unbearable moment. a palpable. interred moment lest its presence make us sick. drag us. a noiseless chain. it could be worse.

whoever comes here to get some share of us. don't ask. hanging by a thread . . . . dragging our shadow behind us on the pavement. it's a fucking joke. smile.

ON THE CUSP OF FINITUDE AND ITS AFTERBIRTH

limit. the present. dull ache.

tell the citizen she must regenerate. be regenerative.

else she can never see her own innermost . . .
else she can never be twice born twice bloodied born bloodied
else she can never hear the words of her own making unmaking
else she can never taste smell feel touch see her own

ere she can see
the right to be in the dark

can you hear for instance the mirror—its rattle—not yet firmly fastened to
the wall

make rice arithmetic aspirin Pierre South Dakota my erstwhile manservant.
Esther's via negativa. her very own motor skills. drawing?

the happenstance of us. or a drain on the clerical system. fuses blown.
fidgeting buoy out to sea. Burbank California at sunset a jet stream.
bending light tubes into henpecked paragraphs. dried up bygones. her
earnings. her earrings. The Grand Canal of Amsterdam.

cedillas. stones in our palms. ojo el piojo. mechanisms nose themselves into
place. place names. exactly alike anew. an avenue's width. leverage to buy a
new one. exactly alike. at least an outfielder's try.

her ink. her john hancock hats off to her manservant. his nightfall more
aspirin a mower like footfall. her knee twitching at night replicates lungs.

RIGHTLY SO MILWAUKEE

being all
being about being not prepared

to see it soiled by confrontation

with the actual
with everyday

not enthroned above distinguished by Attitude & Distance
detachment parenthesizing contemplationizing for Simpletons

It's a fucking joke. Smile. It could be worse.

the dreary mechanical unfolding of objects in the shape of what?

a field fields plane trees. it is waiting for us besieging us on all sides.

the secret glamour of numbers or ends abortively or begins knowing it and
speaking it. revolving it all.

it all

in the unsecret depths of it to the nth degree
not erudite without Substance & Weight with stagnant phrases

extreme burlesque evanescent ripples
the sheepish impact two bodies have upon each other

X THE HUMAN CANNONBALL SUCCUMBS TO OLD AGE

a little light and now raging. central papers and point. heating did the same face diluted in water lead to false doors or blow markets. hanging heads heart beats. how to change i want everything in the partitions of air. listen the sound of footfalls ranging in space which is there. and pivots towards an escape.

it is a frightening dusty weather it is indeed that which is returning. just a minute late at night let someone tell. the strong little breaths live flesh little flesh. perhaps at least they will start up the machines—memory— space twists in an immense tunnel. not spring not a footprint nothing but blue spots at the corner. nothing stays. tiptoe.

the one who waits tiptoes out of proportion out of perspective. tiptoe carcass. rise up carcass and walk. sacrifice one secreted sometime ago secret the spectacle of the eyes. a still life's color. the night decomposed empty upon an empty tongue. twisting toes the puddles and listen for the footfall.

dry bell. the eye hardens. travels. harder to open. hardly open eye in the head that got out of line that has fallen empty. the lights are all out. the secret and same number before the world before us and the incarceration of escape. to pivot. a nail. behind us the turning roads under the space of hard clouds.

am i going to see god mummy? pivot. put your fingers on it. in the streets in parks during the summer months grip the grass between your toes.

Pairing Off and the Space in Between

let's go back to the motel. pivot. just bury me with it whatever it meant she meant she would have none of me save none of me. so i bury myself with her. save her. myself with her bravery. tying up my parts. making me one. her high collar her dark hair sitting there before the window. the hidden dirt under the ledge. at her feet on its back. sighs of remorse. spinning spitting sparks.

the door is closed again unknown to those inside the inhabitants and their quiet murmuring and the wall's too narrow. tracing a figure whose lips are period. no other shelter but space. dilapidated space.

i can't keep a finger on it. be evil be devoid of cruelty be parsimonious be abstinent and weak and modest be a brutal question. domineering on the sidewalk be revealed where are my papers. a tired grown-old question.

where are the dates. a floating basket. the imprecise birth.

who told you to stay there underfoot nothing but dust assaulting dust waiting on a further shore. more modestly fishing around in the mud. a puddle. a rain puddle.

THE CANDELABRA

to put it mildly unresolvable
with your own eyes
murmuring a boundary
dreadfully un

one two three four five florence the place a familiar story one evening.
once vespers as the reader will remember the kind reader gently
remember. remembering whose only dignity whose only sustenance a
stomach could remember and makes that wait shorter. more palatable
more palpable. as we are literally that who distracts us. who knows no
pardon never pardons this hand. something less heroic today between ones
who are working.

conquest too vast. inspecting the figures scores of assessments. given here
under. no map of migrations but arrival at the threshold. acclamation
festivities repose yet the urge toward another departure this time with a
mariner. both appetite and need. me pardons myself.

we have corrected not only our own likenesses but several positive errors
and mistakes. don't turn your face away. unheimlich. dreadfully un. watch
the infrared door count the seconds.

bodies cloaked in light sector 6 sector 9 repeat. please join me.

IRONCLAST WITHOUT BRAKES

broken branches
waterfront footfalls more & more
lost in the fray
urban renewal urban erasure i march in effect
being in effect
being branches

roads of the world. whose world an effect.
dictating a violent principle which keeps on following us back in. our
fashion intoxicating properties over all of us. things which are perishable
navigate through us daily the land parceled out smaller and smaller and
smaller into vast spaces. knowledge thereof collapsed and frayed at the
edges. realty/reality. we will have none. rather or better lingers on an
absentee pretense. kind reader as kind dog reenters and turns the radio on
fetches a knife to better butter the bread. bread's both sides. butter our
feet for good measure make foot prints.

spiraling place following back into itself? a sabotage or insurrection
exhausted resources turns back into a murmur of itself of ourselves.

COLLAPSE INTO MONEY SYMBOL SUBJECT

women feminine or variations thereof emplotting myself against.

indiscreet: speaking not from our mouths but from our genitals.
invaginated writing?

pro and contra yes but the exchange itself? no dead ends but the left-out
hidden the de-emphasized denied articulation set in motion. our motto
our knees hurt.

and when a man says "I am a woman" he is sure of himself.

the erasing of differences to increase exchange value. a genderless mall
with sales on old sporting goods and old food.

in which sense in what sense how to say i or we and in what tone of voice.
her plot is not her own or i mean and the repetition is unbearable.

and of them and her palm and with light with color
we always she did will always
always here she will always
always a thing here an ample question

the erstwhile manservant having come to what indifference. to what
profound conviction of having lost the right track. his own track. her
trajectory. plane trees. he offers non-pareils and we arm. we inflate.

kept alive by primary sources jelly donuts and ermined eyeballs. a circus
clown aristocrat inadvertently conceals his identity to cause the death of
the beautiful aerialist whom she loves. more careless gossip and confusion.
an heiress offers an apron made of newsprint worn by the inflating chef in
the logging camps of convicts.

I WANT A BODY WITHOUT ORGANS

a tunnel perhaps. funnily.
i want a threshold for my filter if differently
i want to work on the paths and impasses of figurability
        unabashedly here
        uncontrollably there
        unheimlichly there and here
on the borders and bridges

the prophecy of doom a modest one a question of local politics
amoeba-like capital. making a process its own possession. menacing
disappearance. smile. effective being. predator's warfare.

the troublesome helpmate. pivot.

stupidity inconstancy irritability frivolity loquacity drunkenness gluttony
hypocrisy perversity selfishness our examples could be multiple. multiplied.

the other's response. paranoia. loss of all boundaries becoming too painful
seeing or even meeting god. say out of joint. warfare's predator.

no longer an isolated system of loans and debts

TO LIVE ACCORDING TO

to accomplish in living a living

to accord with lived accomplishments

to steal oneself away to steel oneself against

to bury some of you with me

to save none of me—my earrings

to guard with our lives the trunk filled with what?

to buy raffle tickets at any and all occasions

to ink self resolvability—dreadfully un

to suddenly become my sex someone else's

SUCH AS SHE, SAY SHE, DID SAY I WAS

if joining may if joining might
fluctuating—combination and refusal
erratic and volatile instability the sine qua non of it
its blood line its lookout tree house

all gender promenade emanating whether from and whoever
not none or neither not unlived not indifference not the 'real'
dexter sinister. manservants joining forces. very scented.

don't be afraid of it. it won't bite. just step up to it—don't touch—and
speak right into it. (there's a good girl.)

LONG STEMMED BROCCOLI

if into other hands
captain to that which having been gone
will let fall . . .

how slowly she moved from afar driving the stakes into the earth. the wood
stone and dirt accommodating each other.

she stood up and took hold of the bunch of long stemmed broccoli—with
her bare hands she tore them in half. the whole bunch and sat back done
squatting in her wine red taffeta gown. and put all of the torn ends into
her gaspingly huge and rounded opened mouth.

what is the rank of beings who can proclaim their own passing?

OTHER GROUNDS

The power imposed upon one is the power that animates one's emergence, and there appears to be no escaping this ambivalence.

The Psychic Life of Power, Judith Butler

social practices
sensuous
immediately and entirely

outside of reach. reaching further again
grow and fix yourself trembling
only a few if you can touch it. keep reaching

unremarked
not not noticed

neither self-evident nor straightforward
our need being on our knees and in need
directly felt seen and known

we are
industrious sprightly
birds with lumps of sugar and
thistle seeds buried under spotlessly
clean tables and china across
the yard basket in mind and hand

between wayward and wayless

war to champion the act the man thought

main thinking instantaneously translated into deed

the order materialized into action

riding westward

a power to obliterate confirms him

in his theater of operations   he appraises

his exactitude of destructive beauties

terrible orderliness an order to obey

by death in deed my dear no response

corrections receive correcting   back turned burned

open wide here comes daddy

expanding agencies mobilizing grounds on other grounds

a ready-made substitute not no ghosts

joining of unlikelies no guarantees not no never

not to mention on our knees again — unhinged?

going to pieces concealed still

immerse ourselves in its night in a working dream

caveway caveway wayward home

to carry out by a mere act of willing

proctoring what was its own great score. piano music tonight. no hope
of getting out of here water water water bring me to your knees. unfix
inasmuch as perfect motions are all circular and multiplying. might be.
an ever changing link as a point of departure. to collect a varied assortment
of necessaries: shoes, a knife, an armchair, fly papers, a telescope, a kettle,
nails, a barrel of flour, another of meal, a straw hat, a compass, a hasty
farewell

gently insinuates a vast bulk against them. abominates. revels here awhile. small junctures. an exotic body left all over the world wobbling toward some impotence some more abominations. forswear and disband themselves sulking again along the meridians. her hull no longer a young bull face down in the mud again. i force the proxy. bend before the kettle's logic. spur and history of weary errors. cast myself down upon that which might bear aloft.

for all you have done, thank you, thank you, really.

with many kindly thoughts and A very Good Wish for

long hours silently guided steadfastly

Nodal asks: points. partial fixations. entangled predicament.
unearthed hull. a phosphorescent light upon the sea.

Muffled speaks: the struggle against subordination has to be visualized. and
then slumps back into her chair unzips the cuff of her jacket for some
breath partially. not willing really to fight and die for this country (?) nor
to create life. more inclusive citizen. but still but still.

New Citizen speaks: a social agent. an ensemble. corresponding to the
multiplicity of social relations. in many ways and means as far as ships are
concerned. precarious forms. that the breakable be made clear among
bones penetrated with love.

Naphthalena writes: 'Twas a moment embalmed
personal distresses no solid certainty
determinations nobody can wrest away from us
grounded in more than its own compass our own

embryonic effigies in these circles. not concentric not completion. impossible motherhood. waiting for it to start hoping. refrain from false starts starts again. associated starts. social agents starts start becoming.

short syllable. the slough of des-pond said pli-a-ble.

then suddenly you see a child or an old man or someone and become disarmed the face appears populated and dimensionalized holes tires garbage filthy water and scraps of metal litter your path it is hard to get around constant obstruction maimed war wounded crawling between lanes of traffic bound by our own funerals sheathed barely visible violence wrapped in torpor never sealed off from the past and the future

circumference was all over us is the then and now of our
person floating in space. after and through the in of it. from
those who. she who was. you who were. a random
statement needs topics including she was late for the third
time. the slow moving one.

talking to oneself as a kind of rehearsal for life. a closed
window or a rowing oar. close to nothing to wanting. the
heaving. your thought. our chance somewhere in between
what we knew and what we wanted listening for it. while
still talking. await to one side aghast. out turned.

the storm we promised as countless as civilians like luggage
in a row with our ears plugged. closed against moving
objects.

Elle says: history teaches us. . . . .

instruments of history: the spear. the lasso. the bow and arrow.

no longer counted: marriage by capture . . . mmm by purchase.

on the fringe engaged in doubtful legality and property. within it parallel
to it or in opposition to it as the case may be—hitherto been unknown to
the entire world. team spirit kicks us harder.

hence amazon citizens alien citizens four legged citizens war citizens

                                        geiger counter moon landing code
                                        napoleon after dinner mints spot the
                                        question thence veil not lifted but
                                        played with even the phallocrat can't
                                        decide on a story sometimes no no
                                        never again limpid air stream a
                                        subway scene exchange of words in
                                        their own tongue

he's come apart, look, for the time being, clutching himself, then myself, in the mud, tying knots for badges and making pledges. deflate. grinding into himself, at himself, clenching his brain in place. in plural virility on the lawn. a mower eclept. clear away the dirt. clean the tools. lie down in mud liquefying abomination. muddy mouths. to save himself.

his urgency, emphatic sweaty in his interest, to get you out of the way during rush hour outside of the subway station, a hand where your tits would be and the other in the small of your spine, hold us like that in some small place people rushing by light getting shorter, smaller and smaller, tries to relax, not so neatly kept, keeps repeating relax, repeat repeat, and rubbing into. jumping over the cracks, breaking mother's back. missing the cracks. breaking all the mothers' backs not wearing out anything.

resistance and exposure

on other grounds
not an abiding term or ground
yes, two negatives make an affirmative
but variable houses constructed
discursive production circular ruins
no advance purchase necessary

the buildings lit at night indigo, with warm yellow lights from windows,
patterned, written in lights, she looks from the window, watches the cars
moving along the highways, in between the buildings, considers how her
own strategies always exceed their purposes, softly projected towards the
buildings.

standing very close. being here and too close? evacuate. push and pull front door awaits eternally inexorable there waiting to rebuild with the battering ram. physical ruins recoil. for keeps. ere quitting. compacted collectedness. don't choke. enormous resolute monster ere bungling investigations.

stand closer please.
you.
to here.

she slams a door. a game of chess. not grunt work. his is what we'll get when. rumbled hollowly resilient rubber. red corpuscles landscape cutting currents. a whirring noise again yawns and grows louder. blank scream overload.

in turning she fell and she slipped on the path to her knees still singing. insultingly shrugging it off. monstrous elaboration. not the right answer, my lily.

we lay down in the moss and rested

evidently we had circled

missing waterways

my chieftain

another main artery

i alone was armed

intent in their. ensemble of others.

events many. thoughts few. less little corpse—corpses. scrambling proof.
possible? and immediately in search of marvels and ghosts.

flattery and divide and rule. spiritual alleged political. pompousness.
profitable skinny legs. it wasn't easy but what is easy?

armistice? unite. along the highways—set out with shrewdness—of the
world.

expelled. un-re-self-possession. held in place. passive penetration.
fascination. emptied out empty place. twist twist twist within recursive
pleasures. exalting carnal particulars.

open and closing his mouth repeatedly no sound coming out. arrives as a
name already always a name with a color a fold-out name in and out.

could you cut the cord please. working in a fantasy too big for that rope.

exercised by desires, climbing the stairs. strange hat strange head making quiet noises.

offering fallibility as a means of achievement.

he tied her up and gagged her in play then for real tried to fuck her but he couldn't keep his dick hard enough for her tight ass moreover school the next day. a report on dolphins. the leather couch was expensive and a stereo system behind glass playing a loop tape. earth wind and fire. thinking how she had told me she wanted to be a bird. nothing to protect. vanishing. flare ups and torn asunder. obdurate pollywogs. sample of articles of commerce. instruments of. grand curves and swoops and blotches. her cipher. a fantasy of fleeing. its embodiment all together. used all resources.

citizen soldier
operation spare change
safety features in tow with pussy willows
search and destroy
reproachment
in both english and french
gameboy's dirty thumbnails
crying babies
in the sky malls
all over the world

trees trees trees
plastic guns
sustain between sustaining

not just the house allegory. not alternative but highlighting existing
relations. an exterior. bringing in the unlinked into the field and that's not
an allegory.

low lands hook hands. nor was it that we survived. coming out from under
the desk
           oscillating noises—unborn yet—crackling microwaves

pontiac lemans malibu a a a small naked shadow ill and crouched
the park flooded small rafts of wood roped to oil cans
we float around avoiding and greeting the sharks

then someone tilts the park. what we get. belonging. having belonged.
                              so now we all live together in
                              a pretty little house. armed hulls.
                              no more trees.

<when i am king

toiling domestic thread slowly stirring vast against household drudgery
pretty domestic

<when will i be king
<when we are all kings
<under the desk

our alpha to our omega
at the present time
trumpet of jericho
c c c c o captain

ask us, ask us anything

          only numbers
               rubbing snow in our faces
          only numbers again

                   no answer
listening to trivia. blindfolded and pinched feeling our way toward a
parade grounds. buried she wakes and ask us again how many.

Pivot says: Let us follow this line of reasoning a bit further. moving even herself.

N says: but we have something to say.

Pivot drives through a stop sign oblivious to the nakedness—unusually. Pivot writes a note later. To say, yes, to say and in so many ways. Pivot returns to the scenery sees N's head with trees flying through her and past. they are more frequent and can't stop coming. Pivot queries: Do you imagine that the trees being so plentiful make too much oxygen? spinning and plentiful lungs.

on the margins of humiliation, recoiled a self-violating turn around, adjoined to automation, irritation, half lives, her linguistic registers, just reading all the originals, on demand and without apology.

abundances contract, i contract in its absences, leaving a refracted trail of what's not being told, not said about us, about you more precisely. leveled against us all. given a drama to act out. shelter for a wayward dog.

it falls, is noticed, at the peril of putting a little aside each year, daily but sluggishly, you are, most cares and pleasures form a rough portrait ebbing inwards. accurate within its own measure. would be again, always ever, in our heads, changing and moving. discomforted and standing exposed. rigid too. the air is there too. not yet still against the inevitable, o sister, the possible.

BLIND SPOT

– Flor, dear. They killed your folks.

*– I warned you not to dig. Every single one of us. They set me on fire too.
I was on fire, I ran after them. I begged 'em to kill me. They laughed. Don't dig,
I said, didn't I?*

Come and See, directed by E. Klimov, 1985, USSR,
a film about the occupation of Byelorussia in 1943.

an ordinary field with ordinary cows nearby runs an ordinary road. but everything must sing the same song. no wrong notes while the watch is kept. the outside husk frozen mud eyes open to the mold. a semblance of a city. the doors are closed. deaf to rhythmic endless cries. shredded imposter. nails. stores of hair. an endless landscape dwelling without.

the suggestion of doubt. a genuine style. to produce a fullness.
we. drowning in our circles of possibilities.
force yourself force others. the time in which.
an insubordination of expression.

talking asking something of the side of a tremendous hole cursing it or praying. time passing but not past. then further in the sand digging a hole into the ground into the sand itself.

relentless inexorable yearning and tenderness leaning downwards. careful not to choke. enclosed with the invisible yet shiny moveable. malleable. turning. starting downwards.

on an island encased and floating in biological sludge. water made dense impenetrable with algae. dear Flor left behind for your shoes in exchange. you the newcomer you wounded your attachments left behind unraveled. no lack of specificity yet seeking more.

no fruits or vegetables so as not to infect. all the trouble starts with their kids. they having them spreading contaminants microbes more moral infliction. a token of our infection.

Flor. stand for yet another photograph. this time (not with the partisans with your double-breasted jacket shoes still intact) but with a gun to your head pointed at your brain dear Flor.

be on your way. be on beyond what makes them bid you to do their bidding. be gone.

they will kill the cows also take the pigs and geese for later. encompassed in black smoke blurring your picture. fire spilling across the road like rain but slower. kicked in the ass for dead.

> exposures and hesitations
> resistance and restraint
> > > the
> > > > specificities
> reflections / necessary links
> > underscore a perpetual
> > > struggle

> not using a prefabricated
> > > rubric
> > > but
> > > movements

> > > > already
> a vanishing point which always

> > always a small door we might
> > > > > enter
> > > > under the
> > > > > clouds

not the last but the last after the last

the well-intended reconfigures that which it seeks to vanquish.
inadvertently. an infirmity without content. striving ever for the present.
the fate of infinitude to dwell in negligence. rusted. trusting resilience.

a stern face. not the newcomer's. speaks with a gesture says. save her for
your pleasure. burn the rest.

the captain's daily conversation.

burn the rest.
leave the grandmother to breed.
she's in the bed in a field clutching a blanket for warmth and protection.
struggling to register diversity and recalcitrance not an impoverished
impression.
she hunts for crude instruments.

resistance to work in work
                    instructions our blind spots their outlines
                    road hazards up to the level of urgency
                    our retaliation making mud soldiers on the shore

happening and making it happen at the same instant. having a stake in
construction burdened but not restricted. a more difficult labor of agency.
a point of departure not an ossified point but emerging from it.

muddy boots stored in a drain pipe in the woods beside a busy intersection.

Flor never returns with the cow to feed the people who are escaped from his or their town to an island excluding the effigy. the cow lost along with the companions are killed in the cross fire light show land mines. the cow sinks to her knees not sure if she is dead yet. cut flowers in water. then dies slowly through the night Flor's pillow.

the newcomer. not digested but kept alive within the flock of pedestrians. gathering in puddles. making mud in hollowed out cavities.

the people on the island made an effigy. a ritual for the effigy. Florian's hair adorned the skull whose flesh was clay. they saluted him told him their problems he had but to listen. Flor tried to put his head in the sand. no one could stop him. Grace seems to have seen glimpses over her shoulder what Florya couldn't yet see: the bodies his family twin baby sisters his neighbors his childhood friend. left yesterday out back behind the houses.

under its tendentious laws. maim existence. paralyze thinking. about time. about change. divorces us from speech. from our speech itself. against the narrow or local ways that construe. construct. make a megaphone out of your hands. reassert the specificities.

Grace wanted to be glamorous a Lily of the Valley from a famous city. but Flor made deaf by the bombs left to constant whirring and oscillations just whirring. whining undertones enacting contents.

Grace aware of her intense femininity. her frustrations. waiting then distraught then destroyed. not about her but to narrate her life as she might have told it. her own reflections on herself following closely. not fatefulness. can there be in us anything which can contain?

they had stolen a cow from a villager who was out behind his small farm
pissing in an early morning fog. a regular morning routine while under
siege. the cow came to be left on her side in the field no promise of milk
nor meat not for anyone. wasted meat and milk and god said to the cow:
the truth gives birth to hatred! as the darkness was overtaking her. the cow
watching the light show. a servant of truth having neither joy in truth or
falsehood. small hesitation small wealth of countenance. she might have
wanted to deceive to play a game on the villager but never be deceived. just
self truth joy in truth. her claim but dimly now standing then resting. the
darkness overturning her. she. servant to none now.

inundation. sutures. respiratory value drinking in. ligatures. we could hear
us thinking. to accomplish the multiple and disarticulated rhythmic
roaring. not portioned but fabricated refusing to be absorbed. that
invitation at least rejected.

meaning's evisceration. self-cancellations self-penetrations. inceptive.

not assured by but exercised. magnets on the heels of his shoes. kicking
stones.

the village had made them supper dinner for the victors while the
newcomer sat amongst them the villagers who were serving the victors
while he sat planning: how to not write their history. of the victors. but the
history as it was being transmitted to him history executed in contract
promise pact from the past to the future to and by those complicit who
anticipated his coming. pledge to write a history. this emergency. the state
of his emerging he has come to be living. theirs. they. dear Flor. you with

them watch the victors eat the food that has been prepared by the villagers. they give them clean linen to wipe their mouths. the soldiers break the windows to ask the villagers for seconds. they give the victors some hot tea. soon the victors round them up with music. a hunting tune sung with yodels burn them live in their own town hall. their lives. make them dance in circles. the dogs barking continuously with the music furious at the constraint. asked to obey. Flor watches. a notion of the present not transition not progression to obey. but arrested coming to a stop. pause. one in which he can start to write.

without enthusiasm without a preoccupied manner without exchange values but to register a vital pleasure looking being vivid. render nearnesses themselves.

Florian's new friend. mentor and hunting pal who charts for Flor a road toward self-awareness. toward becoming his own. is killed. the soldiers strip him naked and tie his hands together around a sign lying flat on his back hands clasped at his chest heavenly rest with a wooden sign pole tied between lying on top of a sidecar. the sign saying "I insulted a Soldier" held by a dead man Flor's friend and cohort and so deserving to die repeating the insult and apology and punishment he is paraded through town sign still growing out of his stomach for all to see. soldier. partisan. villager. peasant. small child. cow. in the town square. they jam the throttle open and turn the wheels all the way to one side. so as if in a new life of his own the dead man on his back pitched across the sidecar of a motorbike now running with a life of its own that gives the dead man a new life of his own and a sign to ride around inexorably. come and see.

a carcass we will be
        and he our tomb
                which we saw in their faces

      half clay like the part you acted
            kinships adoring
            and perish and contract
            unalloyed elements

to linger be diffuse and spread in infinity in your eyes dear Flor. the secret
pact for us to witness. a chance in flight. a tasteless seed. expected and
awaiting. brushing it against the grain. seeing our coming Flor's face
emerges. flickering.